THE
CHURCH
IN
BABYLON

STUDY GUIDE

ERWIN W. LUTZER

MOODY PUBLISHERS

CHICAGO

Developed by Elizabeth Cody Newenhuyse
Interior design: Erik M. Peterson
Cover design: Faceout Studios
Cover photo of city and sun copyright (c) 2014 by Vera Lair/Stocksy (473394).
All rights reserved.

ISBN:978-0-8024-1356-7

We hope you enjoy this book from Moody Publishers. Our goal is to provide high-quality, thought-provoking books and products that connect truth to your real needs and challenges. For more information on other books and products written and produced from a biblical perspective, go to www.moodypublishers.com or write to:

Moody Publishers
820 N. La Salle Boulevard
Chicago, IL 60610

3 5 7 9 10 8 6 4 2

Printed in the United States of America

CONTENTS

Session 1: Welcome to Babylon   5
Finding God in Enemy Territory

Session 2: Conflicts of Conscience   13
Keeping the Faith in a Hostile Work Environment

Session 3: When the State Becomes God   19
Standing Strong While Others Bow

Session 4: The Church, Technology, and Purity   25
The Courage to Confront a Deadly Enemy

Session 5: Transgenderism, Sexuality, and the Church   31
Calling Out the Lies of the Culture

Session 6: Islam, Immigration, and the Church   37
Balancing Compassion and Security

Session 7: Five False Gospels within the Evangelical Church   45
Defending the Faith Once Delivered to the Saints

Session 8: Taking the Cross into the World   55
Shamelessly Sharing the One Message That Can Save Us

Session 9: Jesus at the Church Door   61
Prayerless Pulpits, Satisfied Saints, and Spiritual Blindness

Session 10: The Church That Will Survive Babylon   67
Prevailing in a Hostile Culture

WELCOME TO BABYLON

Read introduction and chapters 1 and 2 in the book

Summary

I'm writing at a time when America is polarized politically, racially, morally, and religiously. Common ground among Americans seems to have vanished. We are angry, hostile, even violent. Someone has said that we are a nation addicted to rage.

Yet it is into this atmosphere of shrill voices that we have been called to represent Christ. The message we have and the lives we lead ought to permeate society and be a beacon of light in the approaching darkness. The church of Jesus Christ is still the best hope for the world.

But how? How can we, followers of Christ, be the light amid the darkness? Much has been made of the failings of the church and of Christians. And, we must humbly admit, we ourselves are often guilty of the sins of which we accuse those "out there."

Yet the church prevails.

I love the church. For thirty-six years it was my privilege to serve as the senior pastor of The Moody Church in Chicago—a church that has had a continuous ministry in the city for more than 150 years. I have witnessed many changes since the days when I was installed as the senior pastor back in 1980. At that time, the worship wars had hardly begun. In the past four decades, several great cultural changes have fed off of each other to transform our society and contribute to the moral and spiritual disarray we see today. The darkness is, indeed, very dark in our modern-day Babylon. Perverted views of sexuality, the insidious effect of technology, and the rapid rise of anti-Christian bias confront the church today. So too, the church is threatened from the inside by false beliefs and wrong attitudes of some of God's people.

But we are getting ahead of ourselves. Subsequent chapters will deal with each of these pressing issues. The message that I want to share with you, from my heart to yours, is that we serve a sovereign God who will accomplish His purposes through us—as He did through Jeremiah, as He did through Daniel, and as He did through the Jews, His people, who found themselves in an alien land.

WHAT THE WORD SAYS

Whenever I think of the church, my mind gravitates to the introduction John gave to the seven churches of Revelation. Jesus is seen walking among the seven lamp stands and He is "clothed with a long robe and with a golden sash around his chest. The hairs of his head were white, like white wool, like snow. His eyes were like a flame of fire. . . . In his right hand he held seven stars, from his mouth came a sharp two-edged sword, and his face was like the sun shining in full strength. . . . 'As for the mystery of the seven stars that you saw in my right hand, and the seven golden lampstands, the seven stars are the angels of the seven churches, and the seven lamp-stands are the seven churches'" (Rev. 1:13–16, 20).

Visualize it. First John says Jesus was walking between the seven lamp stands (the seven churches), and then he says Jesus was holding seven stars in His right hand (the angels or "messengers" of the seven churches). Jesus both observes the churches as He walks between them and also holds the leadership of the churches in His right hand. He loves His people whom He died to redeem. He observes us and, like these seven churches, He commends us for what pleases Him and rebukes us for our failures, but always with a marvelous promise of reward given to the overcomers. And thus seven times He admonishes, "He who has an ear, let him hear what the Spirit says to the churches."

Here's my premise. Jesus loves His people and carries them in His right hand. He who has been given all authority in heaven and Earth has made available to us all that we need, not merely to survive but to thrive in this hour of growing darkness.

We will not go into the future unprepared—if we are willing to hear "what the Spirit says to the churches."

Back to Babylon—the real Babylon, where in 605 BC thousands of Jews were captured by the armies of the pagan nation and forced to trek eight hundred miles to live among an alien culture. And it was not a peaceful journey. Some Jews were killed when Jerusalem was under siege, others died of starvation. Children were malnourished; babies starved for lack of milk. Those who survived and trekked to Babylon had relatives who died during the treacherous journey. Finally, those who survived settled in the city of Babylon, eight hundred miles from Jerusalem and about sixty miles from the modern city of Baghdad.

The prophet Jeremiah records his personal description of the suffering: "My eyes are spent with weeping; my stomach churns; my bile is poured out to the ground because of the destruction of the daughter of my people, because infants and babies faint in the streets of the city" (Lam. 2:11).

But there they were: men, women, and children. How did they survive in a hostile culture? According to Jeremiah, the Jews were subject to "affliction and hard servitude" (Lam. 1:3). Discouragement, despondency, and depression were widespread. How would they react? And what can we learn from their response as we navigate our own "Babylon"?

The first option for the Jews was to angrily isolate themselves from the Babylonian culture and condemn their captors—and who could blame them? Their anger would be justified because of the harsh treatment they and their families had received at the hands of these ruthless murderers. The second—and easiest—was assimilation. Just keep your head down, go along with the culture, and hope you and your family will be left in peace.

But God says, I want infiltration! Don't withdraw—engage. But without compromise; without contamination.

God says He sent the Jews to Babylon (Jer. 29:7, 20). Think about this: The Jews were in Babylon as a judgment for their own depravity, but now that they were there, they were to take advantage of their plight and be witnesses of God's grace to the evil people of Babylon! They were to see themselves as sent there as God's ambassadors.

We, as the church, will never be effective unless we see ourselves as sent by Christ into the world. He prayed, "As you [the Father] sent me into the world, so I have sent them into the world" (John 17:18).

We are pilgrims, out of step with the ever-changing culture—yet we are sent by Christ, the Head of the church. The church is the last barrier standing between the present moral breakdown and total chaos.

QUESTIONS FOR DISCUSSION

1. Do you agree with Dr. Lutzer's diagnosis of some of the ills that threaten society? What are some others you would add?

2. How can we discern "what the Spirit says to the churches"? What gets in the way of our hearing His guidance?

3. Discuss the options of "isolation, assimilation, and infiltration" for dealing with an alien culture. What are the pros and cons of each? What would you say is your church's approach?

4. "Selflessly meeting the needs of others—loving people without holding their sin against them and showing them a better way—has always been and always will be the most important doorway for sharing our faith." Dr. Lutzer gives some examples of people who are doing this. Can you cite any such situations you yourself have been involved with? What about your church?

AN ENCOURAGEMENT TO PRAY

When confronted by foreign armies, King Jehoshaphat prayed, "For we are powerless against this great horde that is coming against us. We do not know what to do, but our eyes are on you" (2 Chron. 20:12). Then when the choir sang praises to God, God gave them the victory.

Let us pray for wisdom to navigate the rough cultural waters we are experiencing. Here is a promise you can claim: "If any of you lacks wisdom, let him ask God, who gives generously to all without reproach, and it will be given him" (James 1:5).

CONFLICTS OF CONSCIENCE

Read chapter 3 in the book

Summary

For some of us, "Babylon" shows up every day at work. Christians have come to me and said, "What do I do in this situation at work? How can I be a witness for Christ? Where can I compromise?" Hard questions.

It used to be that workplace issues for the Christian involved not joining in off-color jokes or using bad language or perhaps calling in sick when you really weren't. But as we've already seen, our nation is far down the road to godlessness. I think of the man who teaches in a large public school system and was told, "It is not enough for you to be silent about same-sex marriage. If you do not approve it and celebrate it, you could be fired."

Sometimes conflicts arise because of state or federal laws. American Christians have had to wrestle with many questions in this arena. A recent debate involved whether Christian businesses were obligated to participate in a national health-care program that funds abortions and subsidizes contraceptives or the abortion pill.

How do we remain faithful with a good conscience and yet at the same time know how far we could go to represent God to a nation that has lost its way? We need the income and benefits from our job. More important, we are called to bring Christ's light wherever we go, and that certainly includes the places where we show up for work every day. I heard about a young woman who serves in a very diverse work environment. She doesn't "proselytize," but she certainly has been open about her Christian faith and how she draws strength from her small group at church. Warm and winsome, she has been sought out by coworkers for conversations about spiritual matters.

But the question for her and other believers in the marketplace is: Where do I, as a Christian, draw a line in the sand and say, "I can go this far, but no further"?

There's a young man here at The Moody Church who is unmarried. He has made a commitment to living a very wholesome and righteous life. He told me that what motivated him is that passage of Scripture in Daniel chapter 1, verse 8—I love the King James Version: "Daniel purposed in his heart that he would not defile himself." That's where we need to be.

WHAT THE WORD SAYS

I want us to just step back a moment and think of Daniel and his three friends. I've read this story many times, but I am amazed by it when I look at it more carefully.

Daniel, of course, was one of a group of young Jewish men whose talents were recognized by the king's advisors, and so they were brought to court to serve the king. They were given new names and fine robes, and treated like young Babylonian men of learning.

> *Then the king commanded Ashpenaz, his chief eunuch [his chief of staff], to bring some of the people of Israel, both of the royal family and of the nobility, youths without blemish, of good appearance and skillful in all wisdom, endowed with knowledge, understanding learning, and competent to stand in the king's palace, and to teach them the literature and language of the Chaldeans.*
>
> (DAN. 1:3–4)

But for all they were placed in favored positions in the king's court, every day they had to walk past the vessels that were brought to Babylon from the destroyed temple in Jerusalem and placed in the temple of Marduk, the pagan god, as a reminder of the fact that Marduk won. What a heartbreak this must have been for a devout Jew like Daniel? Where was Jehovah when His people were suffering?

But they had to lay aside their anger and sorrow and say, "We're here to represent God—and we will do that at great personal expense."

Let's not hurry over this. For three years, these men were

immersed in Babylonian culture with all of its demonic elements. In effect, the king attempted to brainwash them, to indoctrinate them, starting with those new names. "Daniel" means "God is Judge," and he was renamed Belteshazzar, in honor of the god Bel. Babylonian culture held all kinds of temptations, from sexuality to idol worship—and yet, Daniel and his friends did not compromise. At the same time, Scripture tells us that Daniel did his job well, interpreted dreams accurately, and won the favor of the king.

Daniel 1:8 tells us that through all these temptations, Daniel resolved in his heart not to defile himself. In this case, he refrained from partaking of food that he believed was forbidden to him as a Jew. That was his line in the sand, his "here I stand." He said, "I can do all this, but I cannot do this. Here I stand." And as a result of that stand, he became a witness to the king.

Later on we shall discover that there came a point in which these men could in no way serve King Nebuchadnezzar. But God says, "I have sent you there."

I certainly don't want to give the impression that I think we can imitate Daniel and his friends in being indoctrinated with an occult education. My point is that we should never underestimate God's commitment to keep us where He plants us. There is much in pagan society that you can conscientiously be associated with, but there is much that we must stay away from. That line might not be drawn in the same place for everyone. May God give us the wisdom to know where it should be drawn for us.

Let me be clear: Marduk never wins. Jehovah reigns—even when it appears as if we've been marginalized. Do we believe that?

QUESTIONS FOR DISCUSSION

1. *"[Daniel and his friends] teach us that you can even serve a person who is evil if you are mature and know where to draw the line." Do you think this is possible? How? Have you had this experience?*

2. *Dr. Lutzer also says, "That line might not be drawn in the same place for everyone." What would be your line? Do you think there are things no follower of Christ should engage in on the job? What about the grey areas?*

3. *Conversely, what are some behaviors Christ followers should engage in in the workplace?*

4. *The cases of bakers and florists who would not provide cakes and flowers for same-sex weddings are well known. What do you think of their actions? What would you do?*

5. *Reflect on the idea of God keeping you where He plants you, even though the setting might be challenging. Have you experienced this?*

AN ENCOURAGEMENT TO PRAY

Pray for the strength to stand, knowing that the enemy seeks to seduce us, silence us, and make us afraid: "Finally, be strong in the Lord and in the strength of his might. Put on the whole armor of God, that you may be able to stand against the schemes of the devil" (Eph. 6:10–11).

WHEN THE STATE BECOMES GOD

Read chapter 4 in the book

Summary

Throughout 2,000 years of church history, "church and state" have lived in an uneasy relationship. Sometimes they are diametrically opposed—as in the Roman Empire when early Christians refused to worship the emperor and were thrown to the lions. Other times, as in the medieval era, the church became wealthy and powerful, part of the ruling establishment. But let us skip ahead to the twentieth century and Nazi Germany.

What happened there? The state became god. Hitler told the German pastors that they could preach the pure gospel, but they were not to stand against him or to preach against his policies. So the church survived, but only because the Fuehrer allowed it and only if they kept silent and did not openly oppose the government. And of course, some brave believers like Dietrich Bonhoeffer did speak out and were martyred for their courage.

In America, we can point to recent examples of government overreach and threats to religious freedom. And assuredly we must be vigilant when our freedoms are threatened. But let us look back to a time, hundreds of years before Christ, when a few brave believers stood against the state . . .

WHAT THE WORD SAYS

The story is told in the book of Daniel. King Nebuchadnezzar had a dream of a man with a head of gold. Daniel was called in to interpret the dream. He told the king that he (Nebuchadnezzar) was the head of gold; as for the other body parts of the man, his chest, torso, legs, and feet represented other kingdoms that were still to arise. It's one of the greatest predictive dreams of history, and proved to be true (see Dan. 2).

Nebuchadnezzar could not get this image out of his mind. He decided to set up an image of a man (almost certainly an image of himself) that was ninety feet high, set on a base that was nine feet in diameter, and placed in the plain of Dura.

And now for some high drama.

All the inhabitants of Babylon were brought to the plain to stand beneath the tall statue. Then the king issued a new law.

"You are commanded, O peoples, nations, and languages, that when you hear the sound of the horn, pipe, lyre, trigon, harp, bagpipe, and every kind of music, you are to fall down and worship the golden image that King Nebuchadnezzar has set up."

(DAN. 3:4-5)

Nebuchadnezzar became the "divine lawgiver," and with his new law came heightened consequences for disobedience. Those who wouldn't bow before the image were to be thrown alive into a fiery furnace!

Ten thousand Jews in Babylon. No doubt most of them were there on the plain of Dura for the big rally. No doubt most of them did the emperor's bidding and bowed to the image. Except three of them.

Shadrach, Meshach, and Abednego would not bow down. And as you know, Nebuchadnezzar called them in and, we could say in contemporary terms, said, "You didn't get the memo, did you? Let's go through this again. If you don't bow, you'll be thrown into the fiery furnace."

I believe that their answer represents one of the greatest testimonies of faith in all the Bible. In effect, they said, "Oh king, we don't need time to figure this out. Here's the deal, king: we believe our God is able to deliver us, but if He doesn't, we will not bow down or worship the image."

We too have to be able to say, "Whether delivered or not, we will remain faithful to the Word of God and to our testimony."

We know how this story turns out. The three were thrown into the fiery furnace and they did not burn. And God was honored.

They did not burn. And, importantly for us, they stood alone. Think of it: there were some 10,000 Jews in Babylon. Most, it seems, went along with the emperor's edicts. Only three refused to bow. I have known believers who would not stand alone against the state or cultural pressures. They preferred the safety of "fitting in."

What about us? The pressure to compromise our own faith comes down to this: Is God faithful to what He has promised? Is it true that He will never leave us nor forsake us? (See Heb. 13:5.) The question is not whether we will escape the fire, but whether He will walk with us through it.

I want to add a postscript here. Scripture tells us that this Nebuchadnezzar, this evil man whose armies threw Jewish babies against the rocks, ended up believing in the true God! I think he's in heaven today.

You never know whom God is going to save. The person who seems most rebellious, God is able to humble as He did Nebuchadnezzar. And Nebuchadnezzar ended up praising the God of heaven.

I was in eastern Germany after the Wall came down, and a pastor told me that "here under communism, so many Christians buckled under the state." The communists said if you don't give us your children, if you don't go along with the party, you'll be marginalized, you will not be given good jobs, your kids will not be able to attend school. Many Germans submitted and compromised. But some didn't.

In a hundred years, who will have made the best decision?

QUESTIONS FOR DISCUSSION

1. *"A Pew Research study found that 40 percent of millennials believe the government should be able to prevent people from publicly making statements that minority groups may find offensive." Do you believe "freedom of speech" has its limits? Why or why not?*

2. *Dr. Lutzer says, "Freedom of religion in America is not what it used to be!" How do you respond to that statement?*

3. *It's difficult to know what any of us would do when faced with an extreme challenge to our faith. What do you think it takes to stand firm?*

4. *Have you known believers in other countries who did confront such opposition? What was their response and what could we in the United States learn from them?*

5. *Dr. Lutzer says, "You never know whom God is going to save." Do you know some unlikely person whom God might yet save? Will you pray for them?*

AN ENCOURAGEMENT TO PRAY

Pray for the same courage that Shadrach, Meshach, and Abednego were given; delivered or not, they would not bow to the image. They prayed,

"If this be so, our God whom we serve is able to deliver us from the burning fiery furnace, and he will deliver us out of your hand, O king. But if not, be it known to you, O king, that we will not serve your gods or worship the golden image that you have set up" (Dan. 3:17–18).

THE CHURCH, TECHNOLOGY, AND PURITY

Read chapter 5 in the book

Summary

Let's suppose you woke one morning to discover that someone had stolen your children while you were sleeping. They were abducted so silently that you never woke up. You frantically search for your kids while you speed-dial the police. If you had the good fortune of discovering your children unharmed, you'd take maximum precautions, doubling the locks on your doors, barring your windows, and installing a high-tech, ultra-sensitive security system.

But what if we already have a monster in our homes that doesn't steal our child's body, but does steal something even more valuable—the child's soul?

I refer, of course, to technology. Screens. Devices like smartphones and tablets. Social media. The internet. Games and texting and videos and personal updates.

Recently I was at a youth conference. As I looked out over the congregation from the back of the auditorium, I noticed that virtually all the kids were on their screens. And I don't think they were looking up Bible verses, for the speaker had not yet gotten into Scripture. They were probably texting or looking at videos.

Is tech necessarily bad? Of course not. I sometimes wonder how I got along in the days before email. Cellphones are a tremendous convenience. Social media like Facebook enables us to stay in touch with family. Church websites can help those looking for a church. We can read entire books on a screen, or look up Scripture passages, or book a flight. We can access the day's news wherever we are (though that can be a mixed blessing!).

Technology—for lack of a better term—has much potential for good. And for evil . . .

I think there are three myths that we have bought into regarding technology.

One is that technology is neutral. "It depends on how you use it," we say. Well, to some extent, that's right, but technology is weighted against us. Every study shows that technology is almost instantly addictive.

Second, we say, "What I watch doesn't affect me." That's not true. Whatever comes in through the eye, especially that which stimulates desires, affects us greatly.

And third, we believe that technology actually is something that we can control. No, you can't. Its allure is just too powerful.

I could tell you one story after another of children involved in the internet, in pornography, and in video games where they ended up with demonism and all kinds of awful, awful things. Then there is the explosion of vitriol on social media, the anonymous "trolls" who engage in personal attacks . . . the cyber-bullies making some young people's lives miserable . . . the venom that passes for political (and religious) discussions. More subtly, continual exposure to such speech slowly erodes our sense of what is acceptable in public discourse. All this poses a tremendous temptation to we Christ followers, who are commanded in Scripture to speak in ways that encourage and build up!

I believe that when we fight against technology, we are fighting against the devil. That's a strong statement. But there's so much in technology and so many temptations, I visualize Satan declaring, "Here I stand—this is my turf."

WHAT THE WORD SAYS

You know Peter warns us that Satan goes about as a roaring lion seeking whom he may devour. When a lion is roaring, he's not running after prey. When a lion roars, he's marking his territory, and saying this territory belongs to me. And when you think of all the misuses of the internet and social media, cloaked in the appeal of instant communication, information, and "connection," I tend to think that Satan stands there and says, "This is mine."

Does the Bible address technology? Listen to Jesus' words to the church in Thyatira, chiding the congregation about their lax approach to sexual sin. He commends them for all of the good work that the church was doing, but then says, "But I have this against you, that you tolerate that woman Jezebel, who calls herself a prophetess and is teaching and seducing my servants to practice sexual immorality" (Rev. 2:20).

We could think of "Jezebel" as pornography and all the temptations available via technology. Jesus goes on to say, "I will strike her children dead. And all the churches will know that I am he who searches mind and heart, and I will give to each of you according to your works" (Rev. 2:23).

Jesus calls us to purity: "Blessed are the pure in heart, for they shall see God" (Matt. 5:8).

And finally, God's promise through Peter: "His divine power has granted to us all things that pertain to life and godliness, through the knowledge of him who called us to his own glory and excellence, by which he has granted to us his precious and very great promises, so that through them you may become partakers of the divine nature, having escaped from the corruption that is in the world because of sinful desire" (2 Peter 1:3–4).

Think through how technology has affected you. If you are a parent, how has technology affected your children and grandchildren? And then ask this: What safeguards have to be put in place so that we can use technology without being destroyed by it?

We must ask God for wisdom here. And we're in a battle, but it is a winnable battle because Jesus is here to help His church.

QUESTIONS FOR DISCUSSION

1. *"Even as I write this chapter, my fear is that many people who read it will completely agree with what I am about to say but will do nothing," writes Dr. Lutzer. Do you agree or disagree? Why?*

2. *If you are a parent with children at home, what has been your approach to their use of technology?*

3. *On balance, do you think the internet, social media, and devices like iPhones have been more harmful or beneficial to society?*

4. *Talk about your own use of tech. Are there ways you could better manage your use of technology?*

5. *"Walking in obedience and fellowship with God is always a communal enterprise, and when it's necessary to help people overcome the destructive effects of repetitive sin, the church must be available, open, and ready to help." How could your church help those using technology to destructive ends? Is this issue something you talk about in your church?*

AN ENCOURAGEMENT TO PRAY

Pray for purity for yourself, your family, and your church. "Blessed are the pure in heart for they shall see God" (Matt. 5:8). Peter wrote, "Beloved, I urge you as sojourners and exiles to abstain from passions of the flesh, which wage war against your soul" (1 Peter 2:11).

TRANSGENDERISM, SEXUALITY, AND THE CHURCH

Read chapter 6 in the book

Summary

Let us weep for a nation that has lost its way in its understanding of sexuality, a culture where same-sex marriage is normalized and transgenderism is celebrated in public schools. I think I identify with Jeremiah, who said on one occasion, "Oh that my head were waters, and my eyes a fountain of tears, that I might weep day and night for the slain of the daughter of my people!" (Jer. 9:1).

Let us pray for sensitivity and sanity, for help and healing.

George Orwell said, "In a time of universal deceit, telling the truth is a revolutionary act." Let us join together in telling the truth to this generation.

However, if we do not guard our own hearts, a discussion of both homosexuality and the transgender debate can readily lead to a self-righteous attitude among those of us who have never had such inclinations or desires. It's easy to portray those who struggle with gender dysphoria (or identifying with the opposite gender rather than the sex assigned at birth) as somehow belonging "out there" and forget that we're all members of a fallen humanity, humbly grateful for God's undeserved mercy toward us.

I write not with a judgmental spirit, but with sadness. The issue of gender dysphoria is theoretical—unless it's your son who tells you that he wants to be girl, or your daughter who tells you that she's a boy trapped in a girl's body. These scenarios are happening more often than we think, and yes, also among Christian families.

Our churches should be welcoming beacons of hope in a world that is broken. We must compassionately see people who are trying to fix themselves, trying to manage emptiness, pain, and loneliness. Like any of us, they're looking for ways to find meaning for their lives, to find a semblance of peace. And they are going to great lengths to do it.

I disagree with those pastors who refuse to discuss these issues because they think that transgender people and homosexuals exist only outside the church, not within its walls. If we claim that the gospel is for everyone and speaks to the whole of life, then we have something to say about these cultural currents that are swirling around us. Let us walk alongside those who tell us that they struggle with various forms of sexual expression. I have had personal experience with those going through such struggles. Most assuredly, they are inside the church and within our Christian homes. And they need our help.

We in the church must provide these "sexual strugglers" with a safe place to speak honestly of their pain. A place where we listen with love and respect. If all that we do as parents is heap Scripture verses upon our children and condemn them, it will only drive them further into those very lifestyles.

So yes, we hold to the Bible, but we also hold to the idea that listening and communicating and talking without a spirit of judgmentalism is also very, very important.

WHAT THE WORD SAYS

As a pastor, I have had some experience with the reality of the conflict some families experience when gender is no longer conferred by the Creator but is determined by an individual's mind. The modern man says, "If I *think* I am a woman, then I am a woman." And a woman says, "If I *think* I am a man, I am a man."

With an air of defiance, many in our generation say, "God did not determine who I am; *I* determine who I am."

Really? Let's go back and start from the beginning . . .

> *Then God said, "Let us make man in our image, after our likeness. And let them have dominion over the fish of the sea and over the birds of the heavens and over the livestock and over all the earth and over every creeping thing that creeps on the earth."*

So God created man in his own image,
in the image of God he created him;
male and female he created them.

(GEN. 1:26–27)

God created only two sexes who are to complement each other in marital love, resulting in the development of families that populate this world. If you are a man, you will always have male chromosomes; if you are a woman, you will always have female chromosomes. Except in extremely rare cases, every cell in the body is programmed to be male or female. Every person, no matter their sexual orientation, has had both a mother and a father; they would not exist otherwise.

We just looked at Jesus' call to purity with respect to issues of sexuality and pornography within the church (Rev. 2). We must, in love and compassion, share the truth that God intends marriage to be between one man and one woman. And if that does not happen, we need to gently call them to the purity of a celibate life lived for Jesus. At the same time, we as the church must be willing to walk alongside them in what can be a lonely struggle.

Many will object and raise the issue of "unfairness"—why should a person with same-sex attractions be denied the love of a lifelong partner? A fair question, and one that moves some in the church to accept same-sex relationships. But we have to ask the larger question: Was it unfair for Jesus to have to go to the cross to die for us?

Society is filled with all kinds of unfairness. I know a child who suffers from a terrible skin disease. Is it fair? No. Life isn't fair. But God is the one who ultimately makes up for our suffering. As Paul says, "For I consider that the sufferings of this present time are not worth comparing with the glory that is to be revealed to us" (Rom. 8:18).

In matters of sexuality, we have to submit to God. We have to recognize that we are all, to some extent, broken. And at the same time, receive God's mercy, His grace, and also His direction. And let us thank the Lord that we have the privilege of living in this society at this time, to be light in the darkness.

QUESTIONS FOR DISCUSSION

1. *What are some ways the church and individual followers of Christ can come alongside those struggling with same-sex attraction? How can we provide those "safe places" for "sexual strugglers" to speak honestly of their pain?*

2. *How would you answer if you were accused of being bigoted because you are opposed to transgender surgery? Or same-sex marriage?*

3. *How do you respond to Dr. Lutzer's statement that "life isn't fair"?*

4. *What would you do if your teenager told you that a friend of theirs was "trans"?*

5. *We have to recognize that we are all, to some extent, broken. Whether the brokenness is sexual or something else, how do you think our churches and/or fellow believers should deal with broken people?*

AN ENCOURAGEMENT TO PRAY

Pray that all of us would be sensitive to those who are struggling with gender-identity issues. Pray that we would have the willingness to listen, and that they would have the willingness to hear that God honors the body. "Or do you not know that your body is a temple of the Holy Spirit within you, whom you have from God? You are not your own, for you were bought with a price. So glorify God in your body" (1 Cor. 6:19–20).

ISLAM, IMMIGRATION, AND THE CHURCH

Read chapter 7 in the book

Summary

We've all seen the heartrending images of boatloads of refugees escaping war, poverty, and terrorism for a new life in the West. We hear of groups of immigrants coming north as they flee violence in their homelands. Some of us are involved in various kinds of aid to immigrants through our churches and Christian organizations. And almost all of us know exemplary men and women who came here from overseas and have become productive contributors to American society.

At the same time, we must ask: Is immigration always an un-alloyed good for our society?

I find that there is a great deal of confusion on this issue. I've heard even pastors say something like this: we should always welcome those seeking to come to America, because the gospel is open to everyone.

I disagree with a statement like that. The mistake made by many well-meaning people is to transfer the role of the church to the role of the government. But the state's overarching role is to protect its citizens both in the present and, as far as possible to do so, for future generations. The church says, "Whosoever will may come," but the state does not.

The Bible is often pressed into service on the part of those who would argue for what could almost be regarded as an open borders policy with statements like, "Jesus and His family were refugees in Egypt." Or, "God is undocumented," or "We are turning Jesus away." One blogger said opening our borders is fulfilling the Great Commission. But I respectfully disagree.

Today we hear that it's "un-American" to restrict immigration. But historically the United States has always carefully screened those seeking to enter this country, and I believe it is necessary to do that today. We should be having discussions as to what the standards are for people to be welcomed into this country.

WHAT THE WORD SAYS

Nowhere in the Bible does the idea exist that a country does not have the right to control its borders or determine who will come to live within its society. When Abraham left the promised land to go to Egypt, he did so with Pharaoh's knowledge and permission; the same is true when Jacob and his extended family went to Egypt. Yes, Joseph and Mary fled to Egypt, but they almost certainly did so with the permission of those who guarded the borders, and when the crisis was over, they returned to their homeland. These instances are not a model for our nation's immigration policies.

There are several passages in the Old Testament where Israel is admonished to welcome strangers and foreigners (see Lev. 19:34), but these texts are certainly not to be applied to present-day immigration policies. For one thing, Israel lived under a theocracy, and so all who joined them were expected to assimilate by accepting Israel's culture and religion. This theocracy is not to be equated with the nation of America and with its freedoms. Such passages are instructive for the church, but they most assuredly cannot be the basis of the government's immigration policy.

Certainly the state should be compassionate whenever it can, but that is not its first consideration. The state is called to protect its citizens, preserve order, and mete out punishment. Can you imagine a state run by the commands in the New Testament that apply to us as Christians within the church? When a foreign power, figuratively speaking, smites the state, should the state turn the other cheek? Should the state bless the nation that curses it? Someone asked this question: Should the government be compassionate and forgive offenders 70 x 7 times?

There are several references to government in the New Testament; perhaps the best known is Romans 13:1–4. Although most of us have read it many times, we should reread it with new eyes. Paul wrote this during the rule of Emperor Nero:

> *Let every person be subject to the governing authorities. For there is no authority except from God, and those that exist have been instituted by God. Therefore whoever resists the authorities resists what God has appointed, and those who resist will incur judgment. For rulers are not a terror to good conduct, but to bad. . . . he is God's servant for your good. But if you do wrong, be afraid, for he does not bear the sword in vain. For he is the servant of God, an avenger who carries out God's wrath on the wrongdoer.*
>
> (ROM. 13:1–4)

But here's what I want you to understand even more clearly. We cannot run the state by private Christian morality. Jesus, in the Sermon on the Mount, says, in effect, if somebody asks you for something, give them double. What if banks had that standard?

And there is a dark side to immigration. Not all immigrants wish us well. And those are the ones from which the state needs to protect us. The Muslim Brotherhood organization, which is committed to the dominance of Islam over all cultures, released a document that was discovered by the FBI in 2003. This document reveals how immigration is a strategy for Islamic domination—a strategy much more subtle than terrorism.

Of course the great majority of Muslims are law-abiding, decent people. And I've heard stories about Syrian refugees coming here and being shown love and kindness by Christians, and they, the Syrians, reciprocate, paving the way for the gospel. So the church says, "Whosoever will may come," and barriers are broken and Christ is honored.

But immigration is one of those issues about which we in

the church need to engage in respectful, constructive conversation—remembering, again, that the cross of Christ and the sword of the state are two very different things.

QUESTIONS FOR DISCUSSION

1. *Do you agree with Dr. Lutzer that the state and the church are two very different entities when it comes to issues like immigration?*

2. *What would you like to see the government do regarding its immigration policies?*

3. *Imagine you are a church leader. What would you do if a family from another country came to your church seeking sanctuary from deportation? (This is a sensitive question in which all opinions must be respected!)*

4. *Aside from the "state vs. church" question, what are some other practical ways the church could help immigrants? What are some hurdles they face?*

5. *Discuss the risk of misusing Scripture to support a particular position—such as, according to Dr. Lutzer, equating theocratic Israel with the United States. How can we avoid that trap?*

6. *Do you personally have the opportunity to connect with people from other religions and cultures? Can you think of someone like that whom you could befriend?*

AN ENCOURAGEMENT TO PRAY

Pray for our political leaders, "First of all, then, I urge that supplications, prayers, intercessions, and thanksgivings be made for all people, for kings and all who are in high positions, that we may lead a peaceful and quiet life, godly and dignified in every way" (1 Tim. 2:1–2).

Pray that all might be welcome in your church. Peter said, "Truly I understand that God shows no partiality, but in every nation anyone who fears him and does what is right is acceptable to him" (Acts 10:34–35).

FIVE FALSE GOSPELS WITHIN THE EVANGELICAL CHURCH

Read chapter 8 in the book

Summary

We have already looked at the temptation for the church to compromise its witness in the world—to be too much at home in Babylon. Just so, we need to look more closely at several of the "gospels" that underlie those compromises and undercut the true gospel of Jesus Christ—our greatest treasure.

It would be easy to make a joke and say, "What? Only five??" Of course there are other false gospels in the church.

But the ones I outline here don't get a lot of attention. And they can slide into our churches without people really noticing it. Here they are:

The Gospel of Permissive Grace—Let me begin by giving thanks to God that in many churches grace is being emphasized to the benefit of the congregation. Many people have been rescued out of sterile, joyless, and performance-based Christianity when they learn that we are not only saved by grace, we are also daily renewed and accepted by grace. But today we are witnessing a perversion of grace, in what we can call the Grace Movement. Today teachers and preachers offer people grace in advance, even before they are convinced they need it.

In times past, we preached the law. Once people were convicted of their sin, we explained the wonders of God's grace. But today, many preachers say that "God loves you unconditionally" and "God loves you just as you are." The person listening hears, "I can continue to sleep with my girlfriend; I can continue to be in love with my addictions, but thankfully, I am pleasing to the Lord because of Jesus." In other words, unconditional love is interpreted as unconditional acceptance of one's lifestyle.

The Gospel of Social Justice—Certainly we should applaud the younger generation for having a social conscience and living out the gospel through community involvement, helping the poor, the oppressed, and the needy. Christians always have had, and should have, a strong commitment to alleviating human misery and injustice wherever it is found. But some millennials, feeling as if they don't fit with evangelicalism's romance with conservative politics, have devoted themselves to social justice and abandoned the doctrine of personal repentance. Instead they have elevated "social justice" to the status of a more "practical" gospel.

We are commanded to live radically like Christ, committing ourselves to the needs of others, body, soul, and spirit. The gospel comes not in words only, but through authentic, caring Christians who are willing to sacrifice it all for others. But we must serve with a redemptive mindset, always seeking for opportunities to build bridges that will lead them to eternal life. And if we don't see that the message of the gospel as singularly important, we substitute a temporal body for an eternal soul.

The Gospel of New Age Spirituality—Many younger evangelicals do not feel at home in church. They gravitate to groups where they can be personally involved in honest sharing, caring for the poor, and ongoing relationships. They are more open, more vulnerable, and less inclined to follow the dictates of "organized religion." They are a "seeking" generation and uncomfortable with being told what to believe but are committed to finding a faith that is right for them.

Despite many admirable qualities, this generation is open to exploring spiritual experiences independently of Bible doctrine. Thus, in order to be more relevant, New Age spirituality, which is widely accepted in our culture, is often taught alongside biblical teaching in our evangelical churches and seminaries.

We can be heartened that classes in spiritual formation are being offered in churches, seminaries, and Christian colleges. But in many instances, the texts used alongside the Bible are books such as *Traveling Mercies* by Anne Lamott and *An Altar in the World: A Geography of Faith* by Barbara Brown Taylor. These essays and reflections are highly experiential. Such books and others like them are popular because they present God as more accessible, more easily experienced without any need for specific Bible doctrines. However, we have to teach our people that the only sure knowledge we have of God is based on Scripture, which must be believed whether we experience God or not. Martin Luther, the evening before his confrontation at the Diet of Worms, had no experience of God at all. He begged God to help him, but there was only silence. The next day with nothing to guide him except God's bare Word, Luther refused to recant, and we still refer to that event as an important turning point in church history.

My point: we might learn some things about God when we experience the world, but only in the Scriptures do we have a reliable guide to lead us to encounter God and salvation. Sometimes we have no experience of God at all, but "we walk by faith, not by sight" (2 Cor. 5:7).

Contemplative prayer has become a popular discipline among many Christians. Yes, contemplation is a much-needed discipline in today's stressful world. But some Christians are convinced that, through "contemplation," they can connect with God in the soul of their being. And so they begin by "centering," that is, focusing their minds on a word or phrase that helps them connect with the divine within them. Before they know it, they are having a spiritual experience that is divorced from theology and encountering their mystical center, which they think is God. To no one's surprise, soon they are imbibing the general tone and techniques of Eastern religions.

People want spirituality, but not religion—and on "their own terms." Some of the leaders that are often mentioned as authorities in helping people find God on their own terms are teachers like Thomas Merton, a Catholic who was so greatly influenced by Eastern religion that some who knew him well said he was more Buddhist than Christian. Father Richard Rohr is another currently popular author who imaginatively uses Trinitarian language in order to give a backdrop to his own eclectic spiritual teaching. His most recent book, *The Divine Dance*, uses the language of the Trinity as a pretext for describing the "divine flow" in which everyone participates.

This book, and others like it, exalts human nature, our "divineness" and our ability to meet God without doctrine or the teachings of religion. There is no emphasis on repenting from sin or seeing who we are in the presence of a Holy God. By no means is Christ the only way to the Father. After all, no matter your religion or where you are on your spiritual journey, "you are already in the flow."

What is so attractive about New Age spirituality? *At last people have a god who agrees with them about everything!* They want a god who does not embarrass them; a god who thinks just like they do. They want a theology that diminishes the horrors of sin and magnifies how good we as human beings actually are! Self-salvation has many forms and is very attractive.

The apostle Paul has word for us: "For the time is coming when people will not endure sound teaching, but having itching ears they will accumulate for themselves teachers to suit their own passions, and will turn away from listening to the truth and wander off into myths" (2 Tim. 4:3–4).

That day is here.

The Gospel of My Sexual Preference—Increasingly, many churches are welcoming into membership people whose lifestyles flout biblical teachings. Yes, the doors of the church are open to all; but membership (and serving in various capacities) should require more of those seeking to become part of the church.

There have been instances of churches disciplining members who married a same-sex partner, with the predictable result of protests and charges of "hate." The underlying message is: in the name of compassion, the church must never challenge someone's sexual lifestyle. The biblical teaching about homosexuality can be set aside. Jesus was all about love, not hate; to follow Him is to take the path of helping people, not hurting and shaming.

We must distinguish between respecting all people and agreeing with their behavior, between having homosexual impulses and acting on them. We must also counter the widespread notion that those who accept the LGBT lifestyle agenda have taken the moral high road; they, after all, are all about "inclusion" and not "exclusion." They represent "love," not "hate." We as evangelicals must show that these basic premises are wrong, very wrong.

The Gospel of Interfaith Dialogue—Let me say from the outset that I am not opposed to those who engage Muslims in conversations about the difference between the two religions outside the setting of the pulpit. I have enjoyed such exchanges. However, under the guise of tolerance, love, and some would even say evangelism, Muslims are being invited into churches to present a special revised version of Islam.

As emphasized in a previous chapter, becoming friends with Muslims is a privilege given to us by the Lord. And, for the sake of the record, I am opposed to arguing, trying to prove who is right, and expressing words of condemnation. We should not attempt to win an argument but to win trust and show respect and caring.

What I am warning against is "interfaith dialogue," a planned and organized forum that is employed by some Muslims or Muslim groups to present a more palatable version of Islam to a church audience. Muslim participants in interfaith dialogue want an uncontested platform where they can present a version of Islam without undesirable references from the Quran or discussion about Islam's mistreatment of its own people, especially those who disagree with its teachings. On the face of it, such a "dialogue" sounds benign. It is not.

WHAT THE WORD SAYS

For the grace of God has appeared, bringing salvation for all people, training us to renounce ungodliness and worldly passions, and to live self-controlled, upright, and godly lives in the present age, waiting for our blessed hope, the appearing of the glory of our great God and Savior Jesus Christ.

(TITUS 2:11–13)

For you were called to freedom, brothers. Only do not use your freedom as an opportunity for the flesh, but through love serve one another.

(GAL. 5:13)

When the Lord Jesus is revealed from heaven with his mighty angels in flaming fire, inflicting vengeance on those who do not know God and on those who do not obey the gospel of our Lord Jesus. They will suffer the punishment of eternal destruction away from the presence of the Lord and from the glory of his might.

(2 THESS. 1:7–9)

Therefore let us be grateful for receiving a kingdom that cannot be shaken, and thus let us offer to God acceptable worship, with reverence and awe, for our God is a consuming fire.

(HEB. 12:28–29)

For the time is coming when people will not endure sound teaching, but having itching ears they will accumulate for themselves teachers to suit their own passions, and will turn away from listening to the truth and wander off into myths.

(2 TIM. 4:3–4)

My friend, if we believe in the God of the Scriptures, what the Scriptures teach, we must believe even if it isn't our preference. Those that have more light will be judged more harshly than those who have less. But if the Scriptures say it, we must believe it.

QUESTIONS FOR DISCUSSION

1. Since this chapter includes five false gospels, some of the issues raised may need more discussion than others. To begin, discuss the false gospels some in your group may be acquainted with.

2. How can the average churchgoer be vigilant in discerning false teaching?

3. Talk about what it means to "experience" God. What are the pitfalls—and benefits—of such an approach?

4. As Dr. Lutzer points out, it sometimes seems that the LGBT community and its allies have succeeded in painting themselves as more "loving," and the church as more hateful or at least judgmental. How can the church, and God's people, respond?

5. *Do "truth" and "love" have to be in opposition? How do we embody both in our dealings with others outside our community?*

AN ENCOURAGEMENT TO PRAY

Pray for your church and its leaders that they might not fall prey to false doctrines and practices: "For the time is coming when people will not endure sound teaching, but having itching ears they will accumulate for themselves teachers to suit their own passions, and will turn away from listening to the truth and wander off into myths" (2 Tim. 4:3–4).

TAKING THE CROSS INTO THE WORLD

Read chapter 9 in the book

Summary

What does it really mean to "take up His cross"?

We hear people say that something is their "cross to bear"—a physical infirmity, financial adversity, or other difficulty. One of the most sobering realities that I came across as I looked at the Scripture is this: when Jesus asks us to take up His cross, He's not talking about cancer and other misfortunes. I think that what Jesus was saying is this: to take up your cross means that you accept the trouble that you get into because you are faithful to the cross.

As we just saw in our exploration of the five false gospels, today we're living at a time when Christians don't want to offend anyone. So we have all kinds of ways we take the offense out of the cross. For example, if we add works to salvation, we are taking the offense out of the cross. Because it's offensive when you realize you can do nothing to save yourself. Or when you say that Jesus didn't bear the wrath of God—because you want to soften the cross and make it more acceptable. Or we take the offense out of the cross when we say that all religions lead to God, because we want to be "inclusive."

But think about it: It's not really possible to witness unless you offend somebody to some extent.

Note that there's a difference between offending and being offensive. We've all seen Christians who are offensive, and they harm the cause of Christ. So we have to let the cross be the offense. How do we do that?

Let's first look at what Scripture says . . .

WHAT THE WORD SAYS

Make no mistake. The early Christians saw the cross as a horrid reality reserved for the worst of criminals. Crucifixion was not simply designed to end one's life but also to inflict as much torture as possible. And, for good measure, crucifixions were always performed in the most public of places so that the victim would be dehumanized, both by the shouts of derision of passing crowds, and by being exposed naked to the delight of gawkers. The writer of Hebrews captures this when he says Jesus "endured the cross, despising the shame" (Heb. 12:2).

No wonder Paul writes that the cross is an offense (the Greek word is *skandalos*, a "scandal") to the Jews and the Gentiles (1 Cor. 1:23). As for the Greeks and Romans, they thought of the cross as a defeat; no one would want to follow a loser. Even Peter strongly rebuked Jesus for saying He was on His way to Jerusalem to be crucified (Matt. 16:22–23).

But Paul also says: "But far be it from me to boast except in the cross of our Lord Jesus Christ, by which the world has been crucified to me, and I to the world" (Gal. 6:14).

Paul also speaks of accepting rejection without retaliation: "To the present hour we hunger and thirst, we are poorly dressed and buffeted and homeless, and we labor, working with our own hands. When reviled, we bless; when persecuted, we endure; when slandered, we entreat. We have become, and are still, like the scum of the world, the refuse of all things" (1 Cor. 4:11–13).

Jesus left us an example of how to suffer. "When he was reviled, he did not revile in return; when he suffered, he did not threaten, but continued entrusting himself to him who judges justly" (1 Peter 2:23).

We carry the cross into the world when we serve . . . when we listen to others . . . when we are welcoming and humble and respectful and do not yield to strident divisiveness. We carry the cross into the world when we exalt it above political affiliation. And we carry the cross into the world when we witness to our faith, to our Savior, unashamed.

I am sobered by the remark of Jesus that "whoever is ashamed of me and of my words in this adulterous and sinful generation, of him will the Son of Man also be ashamed" (Mark 8:38).

So we must glory in the cross of Christ. It is good news, even for "the vilest of sinners." It's good news that has to be protected; it's good news that has to be lived out.

QUESTIONS FOR DISCUSSION

1. Dietrich Bonhoeffer famously said, "When Christ calls a man, he bids him come and die." What does that mean to you personally?

2. How do we represent the cross in our society? How are we tempted to avoid its offense?

3. How do we hold fast to the supremacy of Christ alone without sending the message, "We're better than you"?

4. Have you had the experience of being offended by someone who was trying to witness to you? What happened?

5. *Paul says, "We have become like the scum of the world." What would that look like for you and your church in today's world that embraces success and status?*

6. *Discuss how we as Christians can truly share the gospel as Good News against the backdrop of a culture that perceives that our light is darkness.*

AN ENCOURAGEMENT TO PRAY

Pray that we might have a clear witness to this world no matter the cost. "If anyone would come after me, let him deny himself and take up his cross and follow me. . . . For whoever is ashamed of me and of my words in this adulterous and sinful generation, of him will the Son of Man also be ashamed when he comes in the glory of the Father with the holy angels" (Mark 8:34, 38).

JESUS AT THE CHURCH DOOR

Read chapter 10 in the book

Summary

Of all the chapters we have been studying together, this is my favorite. This represents my heart right here: Jesus speaking to the church of Laodicea. He is outside the door.

Now if you grew up in a home like I did—a Christian home—you'll often find that this passage of Scripture is used to lead people to Christ. I've heard things like this: "Jesus is at the door of your heart and He's knocking. And what you have to do is open the door and let Him in, because there is no latch on the outside; the latch is only on the inside."

Certainly many people have come to saving faith in Jesus Christ because of that teaching. But actually, in context, that's not what this verse means. Jesus is on the outside of the church, asking that He be invited back. It's the door of the church at Laodicea.

Once I realized that, it changed my whole attitude toward this letter that we are so familiar with. Because I asked myself the question: Why is it that Jesus was outside the church door, and how do we invite Him back?

The fact is that the church saw itself one way and Jesus saw it in an entirely different light. The church said, "We're increased with goods"—because they were wealthy, they were at the crossroads of trade routes—"We have wonderful clothes, we have salves," special salves, actually, that supposedly were able to help those who had macular degeneration, so they said, "We have need of nothing."

And here's the most startling statement in that letter: "You do not know that you are wretched, poor, miserable, blind, and naked."

We do not know! And what we have to do as a church is to open our lives up to God and say, "God, search me, search this church to make sure that You're welcome here." To make sure that we're not deceived.

All of us, I'm sure, are self-deceived to some extent. We may think of ourselves much better than we actually are. But the fact is, an entire church can be deceived. Its leadership is deceived because they see themselves as healthy and well. And Jesus comes along with His stethoscope and He doesn't even find a heartbeat.

WHAT THE WORD SAYS

"And to the angel of the church in Laodicea write: 'The words of the Amen, the faithful and true witness, the beginning of God's creation.

"I know your works: you are neither cold nor hot. Would that you were either cold or hot! So, because you are lukewarm, and neither hot nor cold, I will spit you out of my mouth. For you say, I am rich, I have prospered, and I need nothing, not realizing that you are wretched, pitiable, poor, blind, and naked. I counsel you to buy from me gold refined by fire, so that you may be rich, and white garments so that you may clothe yourself and the shame of your nakedness may not be seen, and salve to anoint your eyes, so that you may see. Those whom I love, I reprove and discipline, so be zealous and repent. Behold, I stand at the door and knock. If anyone hears my voice and opens the door, I will come in to him and eat with him, and he with me. The one who conquers, I will grant him to sit with me on my throne, as I also conquered and sat down with my Father on his throne. He who has an ear, let him hear what the Spirit says to the churches.'"

(REV. 3:14–22)

Jesus begins each of His letters with the words, "To the angel of the church . . ." Who are these angels? Most likely this is not a reference to an actual angel, but rather, the word *angel* means *messenger.* Evidently, each church had a messenger responsible for communication, for getting Jesus' letter to the congregation. As pastors, we should be the first to ponder this letter from Jesus to *our* churches. Rather than protecting the status quo, we pastors have a calling to help unleash the church's potential in joyful and sacrificial ministry. As the saying goes, the state of the pulpit is the state of the church.

And we do well to listen carefully to the diagnosis Jesus gives to this church. He begins by saying, "The words of the Amen, the faithful and true witness" (Rev. 3:14). The word *amen* means *faithful;* it means *truthful.* Jesus is saying, "I am going to give you a true analysis of who you are. My diagnosis is 100 percent correct. I will tell you the truth about yourself—particularly the things you don't see, but things that mean a great deal to me."

Looking more closely at Jesus' words and applying them to our own situation, I believe He is charging the Laodicean church with being too self-satisfied, too comfortable, too close to the prevailing culture, lacking zeal in prayer.

But let us remember: The church belongs to Jesus Christ, and we have to give it back to Him. And we have to say, "Jesus, we are in such a mood of repentance that we do invite You back so that You feel at home here among us."

QUESTIONS FOR DISCUSSION

Dr. Lutzer offers some suggestions for churches to become less "Laodicean" and draw closer to Jesus. Discuss these in your group and consider what these ideas applied to you personally and to your church corporately:

1. *Let us regularly turn off the noise to contemplate God in private worship and scriptural meditation.*

2. *Let us intentionally become involved in the lives of those who hurt, the poor, and the lonely.*

3. *Let us intentionally build friendships within and outside of our churches with those who are different than we are, learning and listening.*

4. *Let us prove the words of Jesus, "It is more blessed to give than to receive."*

5. *Let us give priority to our own marriages. And let us befriend those who are hurting—the divorced, the single parent, and the lonely child.*

AN ENCOURAGEMENT TO PRAY

Pray that God might teach us the meaning of genuine repentance: "Those whom I love, I reprove and discipline, so be zealous and repent" (Rev. 3:19).

THE CHURCH THAT WILL SURVIVE IN BABYLON

Read chapter 11 in the book

Summary

Our worst enemy might be ourselves.

In his book *The Great Evangelical Recession*, John S. Dickerson writes, "The tree of evangelicalism in the United States is centuries old. She is a mighty oak with deep roots. So many saplings have grown up under her shade—trees of education, reform, freedom, invention, work ethic, resourcefulness, wealth and science." But he reminds us that two forces kill old, strong trees: the rot within that is caused by many diseases; and then, of course, there are the storms and forest fires without.

There are plenty of diseases that create rot: the hollowing out of Bible doctrine, the strife between members, and the lack of urgency and failure to feel the weight of the momentous task we have been given. All of this is evidenced by the casualness of many Christians; their stinginess in giving; and their lack of vision beyond themselves. Add to that our self-righteousness and lack of transparency, and no wonder we are not having the impact we should.

What kind of a church will be able to face the unrelenting storms, the floods and fires?

A surviving church must invest in *people, not buildings.* When Muslim armies swept across North Africa in the seventh century, effectively wiping out Christianity, the church was so identified by its edifices, its priestly rituals, and leadership hierarchy that when the armies destroyed these symbols of Christianity, those few Christians who were left found themselves unable to survive. The church disappeared without a trace.

The church can survive without buildings, but not without dedicated saints. Helmut Thielicke once told the story of watching while his home and his church were reduced to rubble during World War II. In his hand, he was holding a key for a building that did not exist. The buildings were gone, but members of his congregation who survived constituted the true church; that is, the people, called by God as a witness to His name. The true church was not destroyed, even by bombs that decimated its buildings.

The church that survives hard times is the church that is

bound together in *community, not crowds*. Not in social media likes, but in genuine friendships and unselfish caring for others. Members stand with each other in good times and in hard times; they are together for accountability, for ministry, and for prayer. The "one anothers" of the New Testament are proof that God never expects us to navigate our way through Babylon solo. Such a commitment goes beyond attending church once a week and then going home believing that one's duty has been done.

Today, there is so much talk about how to make our church services more culturally relevant, especially to the unconverted. However effective this might be in drawing "seekers," it was not so in the early church. Their services equipped the saints to be witnesses wherever they found themselves. The church meeting collectively on Sunday will not win the world, nor will more seminars on church growth; rather, what we need is more equipped individuals who share their faith in hospitals, banks, factories, warehouses, office buildings, and neighborhoods.

We have to change our church philosophy from *telling* to *training*.

I recently received an eloquent letter from a pastor admitting that he was coming to the conclusion that his sermons were not having the effect he had hoped and that true, lasting impact comes from the sort of "life on life" interaction that Jesus modeled with the Twelve. (Who, of course, did not understand or act on all He taught them.)

We have to stop emphasizing an "attractional" model and adopt a training and sending model of church philosophy. That "training" takes time, patience, engagement with others, willingness to challenge, readiness to listen, vigorous questioning. It takes physical presence, a large measure of grace and a commitment to equipping and sending on mission.

Discipleship is not just what you know; it is a lifestyle lived.

The church that survives and thrives in hard times emphasizes *prayer, not programs.* Praying as a united body for the things on God's heart, as the Concert of Prayer movement has done globally, exemplifies how corporate prayer that uses Scripture and emphasizes spiritual needs, along with different modes of intercession, can make our time meaningful and joyful.

We need to share *hard truths, not positive suggestions.* We need to take seriously Jesus' call to repentance, as we saw in the preceding chapter. We need to look at what Scripture says about suffering and persecution; we need to learn from the early church as well as the church worldwide today.

And the church that survives in Babylon is one whose members accept their lot with both sorrow but also a joy that is inexplicable. It is a church that seeks to silence its critics by its authenticity and commitment to others; a church that *looks without, not just within.* It is a church that is willing to follow Jesus all the way to the cross.

WHAT THE WORD SAYS

Fear not!

Jesus said, "Fear not, little flock, for it is your Father's good pleasure to give you the kingdom" (Luke 12:32). Jesus said, "I am sending you out as sheep in the midst of wolves" (Matt.

10:16). But we have a Shepherd who cares for His church.

Jesus said, "You are the light of the world" (Matt. 5:14). And, of course, He is the Light, but we are the light of the world. And a light is not visible unless it is a time of darkness. So let our lights shine that people may see our good works and what we believe and may glorify God in the midst of our contemporary situation. That's Christ's will for the church.

And if I could leave a thought with you that I want to have burned into your soul, it is this: Jesus who gave His life for the church will never forsake us; He will never leave us behind; He will never leave us without protections despite the persecution; He will come through at the time of need. And my dear friends, it is His church, not ours. So be encouraged!

QUESTIONS FOR DISCUSSION

Talk about Dr. Lutzer's ideas for being the church that survives and even thrives in Babylon:

1. Community, not crowds

2. Training, not telling

3. Prayer, not programs

4. Hard truths, not positive suggestions

5. Look without, not within

AN ENCOURAGEMENT TO PRAY

Pray that we will be faithful, even if not "successful." Ask God to show us what it means to trust Jesus who declared that the church belonged to Him, and He would build it (Matt. 16:18). Pray that we will be ready to survive the storms that are already on their way.

HOW DO WE LIVE FAITHFULLY IN A CULTURE THAT PERCEIVES OUR LIGHT AS DARKNESS?

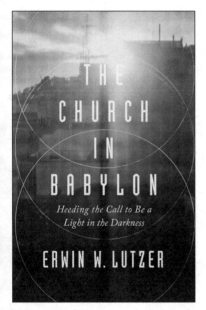

978-0-8024-1308-6
also available as an eBook

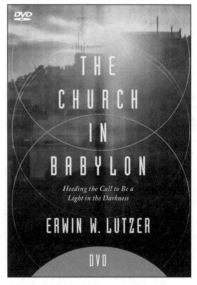

978-0-8024-1355-0

Dr. Lutzer will walk you through the many parallels between the church in America and God's people in Babylon. Then he'll explain what we can learn from the Israelites about maintaining our faith in the midst of a pagan culture.

More books by Erwin W. Lutzer

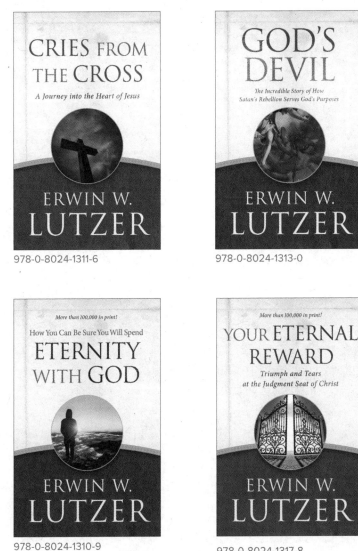

CRIES FROM THE CROSS

A Journey into the Heart of Jesus

ERWIN W. LUTZER

978-0-8024-1311-6

GOD'S DEVIL

The Incredible Story of How Satan's Rebellion Serves God's Purposes

ERWIN W. LUTZER

978-0-8024-1313-0

More than 100,000 in print!

How You Can Be Sure You Will Spend ETERNITY WITH GOD

ERWIN W. LUTZER

978-0-8024-1310-9

More than 100,000 in print!

YOUR ETERNAL REWARD

Triumph and Tears at the Judgment Seat of Christ

ERWIN W. LUTZER

978-0-8024-1317-8

also available as eBooks

MOODY Publishers®

From the Word to Life®

"One minute after you die you will either be elated or terrified. And it will be too late to reroute your travel plans."

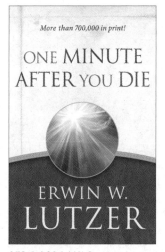

978-0-8024-1411-3
also available as an eBook

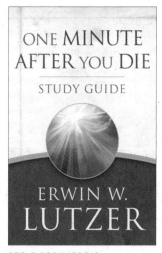

978-0-8024-1296-6
also available as an eBook

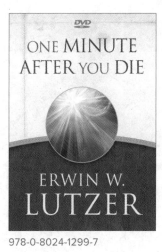

978-0-8024-1299-7

MOODY
Publishers®

From the Word to Life®